DK READERS is a compelling reading programme for children. The programme is designed in conjunction with leading literacy experts, including Cliff Moon M.Ed., who has spent many years as a teacher and teacher educator specializing in reading. Cliff Moon has written more than 160 books for children and teachers. He is series editor to Collins Big Cat.

Beautiful illustrations and superb full-colour photographs combine with engaging, easy-to-read stories to offer a fresh approach to each subject in the series. Each DK READER is guaranteed to capture a child's interest while developing his or her reading skills, general knowledge, and love of reading.

The five levels of DK READERS are aimed at different reading abilities, enabling you to choose the books that are exactly right for your child:

Pre-level 1: Learning to read
Level 1: Beginning to read
Level 2: Beginning to read alone
Level 3: Reading alone
Level 4: Proficient readers

The "normal" age at which a child begins to read can be anywhere from three to eight years old. Adult participation through the lower levels is very helpful for providing encouragement, discussing storylines and sounding out unfamiliar words.

No matter which level you select, you can be sure that you are helping your child learn to read, then read to learn!

DK

LONDON, NEW YORK, MUNICH,
MELBOURNE, AND DELHI

Series Editor Deborah Lock
Designer Jacqueline Gooden
Art Director Martin Wilson
Pre-production Francesca Wardell
Jacket Designer Natalie Godwin

Reading Consultant
Cliff Moon M.Ed.

First published in Great Britain by
Dorling Kindersley Limited
80 Strand, London WC2R 0RL

Copyright © 2013 Dorling Kindersley Limited
A Penguin Company

10 9 8 7 6 5 4 3 2 1
001-187467-July 2013

A CIP catalogue record for this book
is available from the British Library

ISBN: 978-1-40938-175-4

Colour reproduction by Colourscan, Singapore
Printed and bound in China by L.Rex Printing Co., Ltd.

The publisher would like to thank the following for their kind permission to
reproduce their photographs:
(Key: a-above; b-below/bottom; c-centre; f-far; l-left; r-right; t-top)
3 **Getty Images:** Asia Images. 4 **Corbis:** Peter Burian (c); Thomas Marent /
Visuals Unlimited (tl). **Getty Images:** Art Wolfe / Stone (b). 5 **Corbis:** DLILLC
(tr); Visuals Unlimited (c). 6-7 **Getty Images:** Asia Images. 6 **Photolibrary:**
Jurgen & Christine Sohns / FLPA (br). 7 **Corbis:** Thomas Marent, / Visuals
Unlimited (t). **Getty Images:** Daniel Berehulak / Staff / Getty Images News
(br). **Photolibrary:** Stockbrokerxtra Images (bc). 8 **Corbis:** Thomas Marent /
Visuals Unlimited (br). **Getty Images:** Thomas Marent / Visuals Unlimited (br).
Getty Images: Luciano Candisani / Minden Pictures (c). **Photolibrary:** Terry
Whittaker / FLPA (bc). 10 **Dreamstime.com:** Lasse Kristensen (c). **Getty
Images:** Creative Crop / Digital Vision (cr); Ultra.F / Digital Vision (cb). 11
Getty Images: Rubberball / Erik Isakson. **Photolibrary:** Stockbrokerxtra Images
(bc). 12-13 **Photolibrary:** Juniors Bildarchiv. 13 **Getty Images:** Pete Mcbride /
National Geographic (bl). **Photolibrary:** Juergen und Christine Sohns (crb). 14
Getty Images: Gerry Ellis / Minden Pictures (t). 15 **Corbis:** Herbert Kehrer (br).
Getty Images: Ingo Arndt / Minden Pictures. **Photolibrary:** Cyril Ruoso (bl).
16-17 **Getty Images:** Piotr Naskrecki / Minden Pictures. 16 **Getty Images:** SA
Team / Foto Natura / Minden Pictures (bl); Kevin Schafer / Minden Pictures
(br). 17 **Getty Images:** Stan Osolinski / Oxford Scientific (br). **Photolibrary:**
Juniors Bildarchiv (bl). 18 **Getty Images:** Reinhard Dirscherl / WaterFrame (bl).
18-19 **Photolibrary:** Luiz C Marigo. 19 **Getty Images:** Reinhard Dirscherl /
WaterFrame (bc); Claus Meyer / Minden Pictures (bl). 20 **Science Photo
Library:** Chris Hellier (clb). 20-21 **Alamy Images:** Chris Hellier. 21 **Getty
Images:** Christian Kober / Robert Harding World Imagery (bc); Thomas
Marent / Minden Pictures (br). **Photolibrary:** Nick Garbutt (bl). 22 **Getty
Images:** Keren Su / Photodisc (t); Tier Und Naturfotografie J & C Sohns / The
Image Bank (bl). 23 **Getty Images:** Ben Cranke / The Image Bank; Lori Epstein
/ National Geographic (br). 24 **Corbis:** Peter Burian (c). **Getty Images:** Brooke
Whatnall / National Geographic (bl). 25 **Corbis:** Anup Shah (bl). **Getty
Images:** Fuse (br); Copyright Tony Franco / Flickr. 26-27 **Getty Images:** Visuals
Unlimited, Inc. / John Abbott. 26 **Photolibrary:** Michel & Christine
Denis-Huot (t). 27 **Corbis:** DLILLC (br). **Getty Images:** Steve Allen /
Photodisc (bc); Ben Cranke / The Image Bank (bl); 28-29
Wendelboe / Lonely Pl

DK READERS

LEARNING
TO READ
pre-level
1

Petting Zoo

DK

A Doring Kindersley Book

What kind of animal

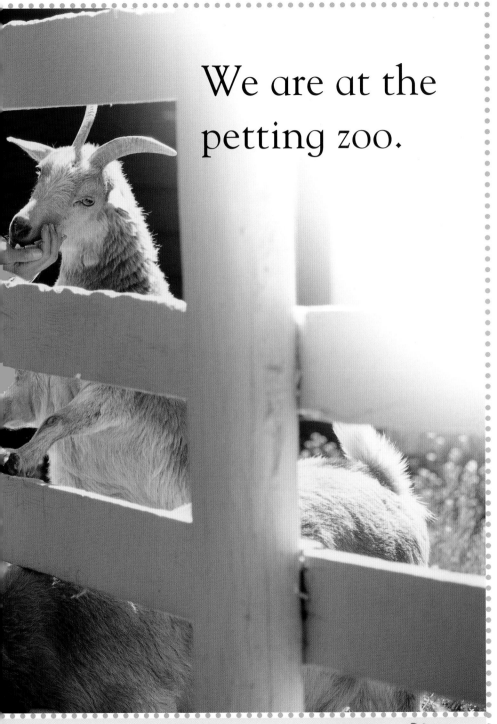

We are at the
petting zoo.

o you see here?

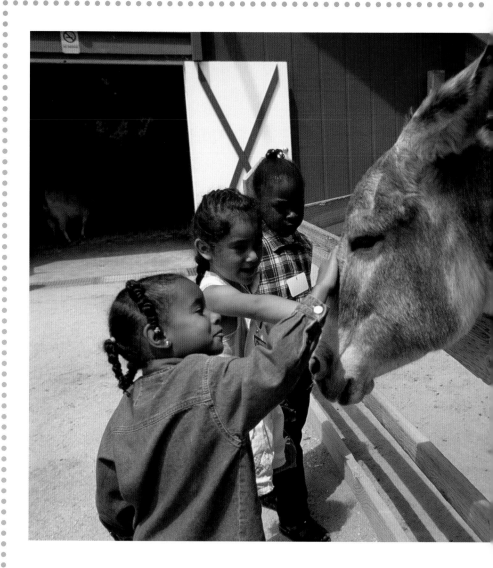

We are petting
a drowsy donkey.

  donkeys

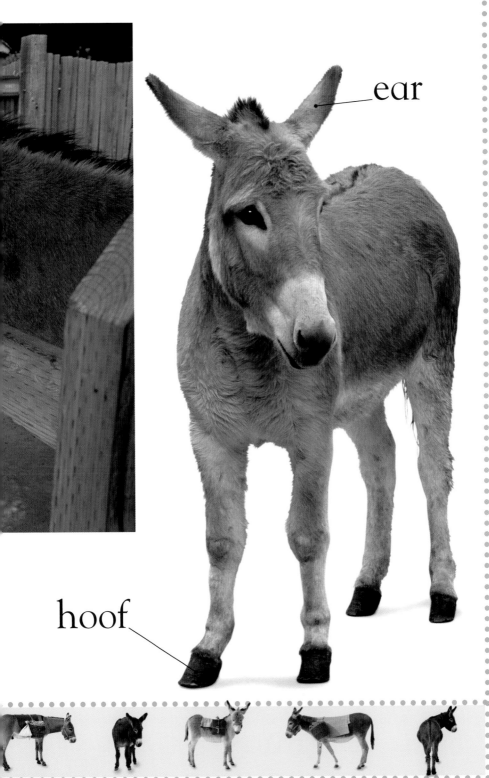

ear

hoof

We are walking two baby llamas.

llamas

lead

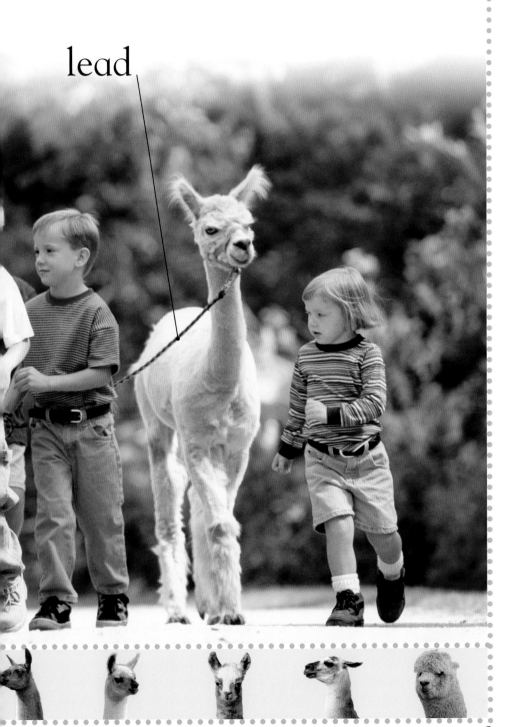

I am brushing
a pony's coat.

mane

 ponies

pigs

I am picking up
a little pink pig.

snout

hoof

hen

 chicks

I am carrying
a soft yellow chick.

chick

stick insects

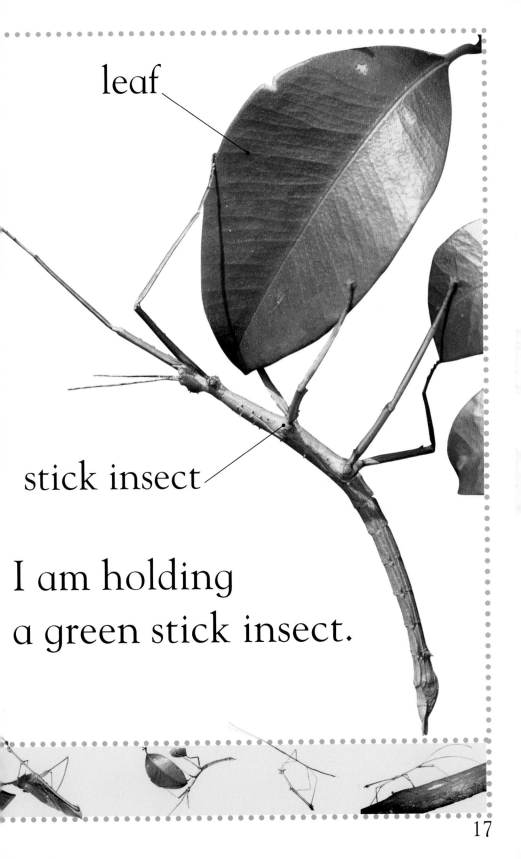

leaf

stick insect

I am holding
a green stick insect.

17

frogs

I am watching
a beady-eyed frog.

Ribbit! Ribbit!

toe

It is mealtime now.
I give the woolly lamb
some milk.

 lambs

wool

I am feeding
a hungry rabbit.

ear

carrot

rabbits

This fluffy guinea pig
is nibbling a leaf.

 guinea pigs

whiskers

claws

The white goose wants a snack.

  geese

gosling

bill

feathers

goats

This long-horned goat is eating his lunch.

horn

Goodbye, animals!

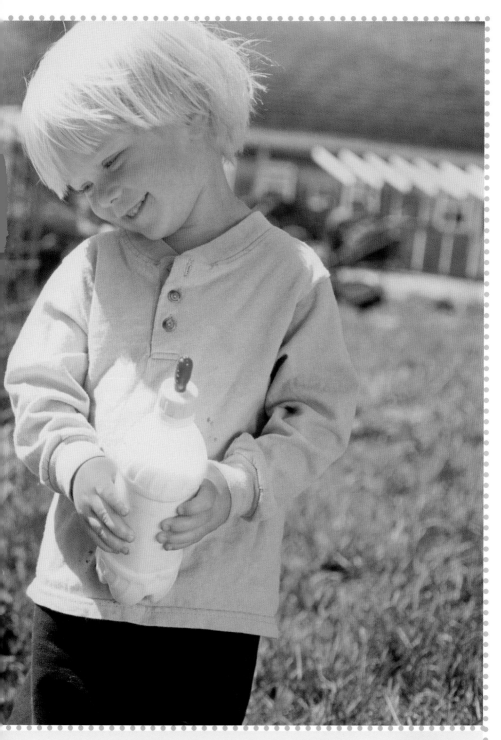

t's time to go home.

Glossary

 Donkey
a small horse-like animal with long ears

 Frog
a short animal with long back legs

 Goose
a large white bird with a long beak

 Llama
a large woolly animal from South America

 Stick insect
a long thin insect that looks like a stick